Just/More

poems by

Martin Wiley

Finishing Line Press
Georgetown, Kentucky

Just/More

Copyright © 2022 by Martin Wiley
ISBN 978-1-64662-733-2 First Edition
All rights reserved under International and Pan-American Copyright Conventions. No part of this book may be reproduced in any manner whatsoever without written permission from the publisher, except in the case of brief quotations embodied in critical articles and reviews.

ACKNOWLEDGMENTS

"Black diamonds and pearls." (Printed here as "10") *Philadelphia Stories*
"Hope." (Printed here as "14"). *Healing Verse Poetry Line*. Recorded by the author.
"My son's eyes." (Printed here as "2") *Brushfire Literature & Arts Journal*
"So base a hue?" (Printed here as "5") *Ponder Review*
"You'll always be baby to me…" (Printed here as "7") *A More Perfect Union: Celebrating the 50th Anniversary of Loving v. Virginia*. Asian Arts Initiative, Philadelphia. Text printed on canvas

Publisher: Leah Huete de Maines
Editor: Christen Kincaid
Cover Art: Martin Wiley
Author Photo: Tammy Bradshaw, Tammy Bradshaw Photography
Cover Design: Elizabeth Maines McCleavy

Order online: www.finishinglinepress.com
also available on amazon.com

Author inquiries and mail orders:
Finishing Line Press
PO Box 1626
Georgetown, Kentucky 40324
USA

Table of Contents

1. 1

2. 3

3. 4

4. 6

5. 16

6. 18

7. 19

8. 21

9. 22

10. 23

11. 24

12. 27

*"Your face is just like the sun when it raises
Thank you for adding beauty to my phrases…"*
The Coup

*to Christy, for believing
&
to Itzela & Elio, for being*

1.

They placed you in my arms and to be honest
I panicked. That little face, scrunched up, mouth scarcely
anything at all, yet the roar you unleashed
rattles within me today.

Your mother said I should speak to you, that you
would recognize my voice from late-night poems performed
against the backdrop of her belly and I thought
it was more happy midwife talk but somehow

as always she knew better—I would love to say I told you of
the deep mysteries or even my worst Dad jokes but I remember
only the sudden calmness

that unfurled itself across your tiny face and it was instantly
clear, so clear
that you knew me, that you
had always known me, and I held you to me and gently
touched your chest to feel
for the very first time my own blood pushed
by another's heart and when I saw myself in your eyes I knew
it did not matter what words I spoke.

I have doubted so much of myself.
I have been afraid of the world, and all its insane demands.
My backstory is a mess, and I have lost myself in hate, and
regret. There are those who hurt me who I did not even know,
and others that I knew too well. But who's to say if just one
smile replaced a sneer, an instant of silence replaced
a slur, if belonging
replaced the loneliness, if family replaced the coldness, would I have
ended here mirrored in newly wide blue eyes?
I do not know if I have it in me to forgive
the world

for my life
but with you Itzela
I was finally able to accept it.

2.

My son's eyes
at seven are wide, wide like
rivers and wide like
singing woods at dawn,

and they blossom, they blossom like
sunflowers shimmering in early morning's dew,

they dance, they dance because they are,
because they are sparkling comets gleefully
traveling lightyears just for a chance
to gently kiss your smile, your heart.

They are
joyous volcanoes, they are
joyous volcanoes overflowing and melting
everything they see.

They are brown, they are the color
of my soul, they are brown and they are alive

and I
have to search inside his eyes,
I have to study, I have to
watch,
watch for that ticking, for that twisting,

for that silent unmarked shifting,
for that moment when
this world no longer notes
the soft brown tones in his eyes,
only the angry brown tones on his skin.

3.

Mornings have become a heavy weight—
eventually getting up and
facing notifications on the phone and
finding brand new holes in the heart and
fearing too many sobbing posts on my timeline—

as a kid I was told knowing is half the battle but
        they forgot to say it's always been the hurting half—I didn't
        want to know
        how we died last night.

I simply wanted to wake up to big brother sun and
take a moment to rest my soul
on a porch swing and
        listen to those precious few happy Nina Simone songs,
        get ready to dance and to live and

        to just be.

The existential exhaustion of fury
is the part most difficult to explain to those
that don't know, to those
that don't carry it inside
their chest.

This system does all it can to break
        Black bodies, to shatter
        already wounded minds, and then make certain

        to stomp any pieces
        that dare rage in their face, those
        dying souls

that risk existing where
prying eyes can see
what the living strained
to hide.

They spy us
    at our worst—

once we have nothing left to lose and
    I'll never understand
    what they think to gain by
    putting us out of their misery.

Even so, these protests will continue, and
those tears will wash
    fresh blood
    from our cheeks, and we—
    bearing timeless shoulders
    that Atlas could only envy—

    we
    will lift that weight
    just one more time,
    just one more day,
    and take
    just one more step—

    we know no other way.

4.

i.

At the last minute I made it into the room, which listed something called "Writing From The Roots."

Series of writing workshops, Celebration of Black Arts, and I decided this one called out to me.

Okay, I thought.

Let's talk about ancestors, maybe check in on ancient rhythms and sacred missions, feel

where we were and what we should have become.

I felt so Black, really, it was lovely.

ii.

I rediscovered
the world within the tangles
of my children's hair.

iii.

The program was already starting; the room was completely
packed. Ducked in, trying to avoid being seen, but

searching for a seat I
could feel disbelieving eyes
as they studied me.

The host began her talk, glanced
at me, lost her place, patted her 'fro,

took a breath, checked her notes,
and started over.

A large woman with an elegant headwrap
leaned to her girlfriend and whispered a laugh;

girlfriend shook her locks
in embarrassed amusement, and locked

eyes with another in the corner who wore
matching smile beneath a rainbow of

braids and twists that danced
down her cheeks.

Well, fuck,
I thought.

And I felt
                    so Black.

iv.

When in touch with our hair,
the host said,

we are in touch with our home, with our
beginning.

The room smiled, nodded, shared unspoken
mutual understandings that,
as far as I knew, were transmitted from follicle to
follicle, borne on waves of cocoa butter and organic Black-owned
locally produced detanglers.

Our roots,
she said,
remain the simplest way back to our roots.

My hands leapt
to my bald head, this barren land where dreadlocks

went to die. I
rocked them for a little while then my

hairline retreated, surrendered a battle I
hadn't even known we were fighting, at which time I

decided discretion, and a newly purchased set
of clippers, remained the better part of valor.

v.

The first time some old White lady reached
for Itzela's hair, grin spreading
from paper-thin lips to knobby fingertips,
Columbus in a peach skirt stalking the line at the Costco,

I did not hesitate to cuss her ass out. I will carry
        her shook face with me everywhere I go—sometimes
        I flip to that page in my mental scrapbook, but
        I promise it's only
        when I am in desperate need of a relieving chuckle.

There were decades displayed in that profanity, infinite moments
when I forced myself to duck my head to accept
        that pat on the head, that fingering of
        youthful hair, all of the uncountable times no one spoke
        in my defense when I was expected to smile
        at the compliment
        of being called exotic.

Christy told me I was rude, that the lady meant
        no harm, and I said

"Meaning's a tricky thing,
        often doesn't matter much as we want to think it does."

We had a good fight about it, speaking firmly but
        softly, under our breath as if worried the toddler would
        pick up what we were throwing down.

But no, Itzela sat, pudgy legs popping out
those kid-sized holes in the shopping cart seat,
soft-serve ice cream spreading
        from plump lips to chubby fingertips,

hair untouched and unrivaled,
>   undiscovered, and for that day at least
>   remaining
>   theirs alone.

vi.

Green eyes hid in a pale Black face
underneath thick brown hair flecked with blonde,
    first a basic short cut then a ragged mess and on to the
inevitable high-top
        fade which led to those 90's sides shaved with that small plot
        of thin dreadlocks up top,
most days my hair was the Blackest thing about me and
ain't that some shit
        —until summer would hit and the sun would darken my skin
but then
        quick betrayal he would seize those flecks of blonde in my
hair and
        stretch them into rivers of gold and now no one knew
        what I was supposed to be

and while that's a question no child should be asked—I learned
        to live with it or at least
        alongside it.

vii.

Something hides within miles of curls,
tucked away in rippling gold and amber and black streams of hair,
    unkempt locks that lock away a deeper knowledge of myself,
    of who I once was before
    I knew myself.

They flow so freely, these strands atop their heads
    and these children running so wild beneath them.

My children know who they are
in ways that I cannot understand well enough to envy.
My grey skin was a trap as a child, defining me and yet
leaving me impossible to comprehend—anti-camouflage, my blend
prevented me from ever blending in.

Older, angrier, I swore in shrieking tones
that I did not care, that I did not want what I so clearly
would never get.

It is those wounds we refuse to admit to
that slice the deepest,
that
bleed

the longest.

viii.

My children' skin glows and I don't know
if the shine comes from inside them
        or if we have simply succeeded
        in keeping grime of the world
        from clouding the blended perfection of their tones,

and yeah I know I failed to find my roots within my roots,
but I have buried my past
within the sprouted glories of my children's present,
and if they can be beautiful
then why not me,

        why not me?

ix.

I recovered my
self through blended roots of my
children's tangled hair.

5.

Hidden to survive, there is death in my blood.

There is no simplicity in people like me,
        no people like me,
        too many people in me.
The sins of my father end in me.
I have no choice but to explain
to my own children how mixed skin
is a pre-existing condition,

& I can tell them that they deserve better &
        that we should have been better. I fed
        myself on Aaron's rage, I feared
        myself in Sethe's grief, but you both

will write your own pages, new songs meant to be sung
        not shouted. Your presence altered
        my existence—drag me to the altar
        of Mount Moriah & I know now
        which way my knife would point. Pray

to the devils; the gods have given us over. They
        wanted this & I
        have brought you unknowing to a world that will
        question your beauty, that will
        proclaim grey so base a hue, that will
        mock your resolve, that will
        burn
        before admitting you've won. It does not deserve you
        & I cannot let myself
        wonder if I've failed you by
        making you.

The echoes of trauma stay deafening but somehow my fury
		did not become hate,
		did not crawl inside & eat through the bones on its way out.

Somehow I found my glory & somehow
		that was enough & now
		I no longer understand how blood
		spills its own blood. I fight to wake
		from nightmares of looking for myself in a mirror & seeing
		only my birth father's Black fingers stained red. But those

aren't my knuckles,
& that isn't my fist. The rage

		remains, though, and the hands
		are clenched—always.

Tell America from me, I am of age
		to keep mine own, excuse it how she can.

6.

We both speak this country's name
—in the space between what you say
         and what I hear
lies the only true definition
of America.

7.

I wondered what you felt
when you were holding

my hand on the way to school, or dragging me
through department stores.

(It was a question beyond asking.)

Even in the mall's dull
fluorescent light I
could tell that my
hand wasn't so much darker than
yours. It wasn't

something I even noticed
at home.

The skin tone on your fingers didn't matter
when they were fixing me a peanut butter and

jelly sandwich. A South Bronx Italian accent
was essentially irrelevant

to a child being sent to bed without desert.
At home, I was your son.

It was only at that mall,
at the diner,

at the grocery store,
that I remembered to wonder

if you ever knew how much I
sometimes

wanted to drop
your hand,

and how
frightened I was that

someday, you
would let me.

8.

You looked so small,
you looked so small and I was so scared and
there was too much going on I couldn't understand.

You seemed so small and brand-new and there were wires and
tubes and machines, each breath
heartbeat
moment
watched monitored recorded,

you felt so small and I was so scared and I thought
I had known what to expect—I'd been here before but you
blazed your own path into life, forced

your way with a wiggle a yawn a snuggle,
you were the only one who never seemed to mind what had to be done,

and eventually it became clear to me, so clear
to me that you
had never been small,

but I had to grow
before I could see all of you.

9.

"You snapped at your little brother,"
I say to Itzela. I take shaky paint-stained fingers,
hold them tight. Kiss trembling fingertips.
"But I'm guessing," I say,
"he's not really the one you're mad at."

And now I am falling,
falling
into razor sharp blue eyes, mirror images of my own but
brighter, fiercer, newer, more hurting yet so much more
forgiving.

"I know," they say,
trying but for once failing at smiling.

"It's just—"

They stop and
I wait.

"There's just…"

"Everything?" I say.

"Yeah," they say, and
they fill my lap

with eleven years of worry, of fear, of grief for things
they do not yet understand,
for things they do not yet understand,

for things I do not yet know how
to make them understand.

10.

He tells me of days when even dreams can't wriggle free.

I see him struggle to hold
the laughing child

once alive inside him,
watch him strain to remember
how beautiful it can feel to be gentle.

There are walls and there are walls,

and now I only see him through gun-proof double-thick glass,
in this place where chained hearts steadily drip
onto already stained concrete floors,
and I don't waste time telling him

I miss him. I find ways to smile,
even manage to drag an actual laugh through his
ragged lips, and his fingers

aren't too torn
when they line up mirror-image of mine. He worries, you see,
that I will let go of even this, and I can offer no reassurance

for that same fear has already seized
my own broken heart.

11.

I will tell you
it was simpler when I could stay
angry, when I could avoid admitting
fear, when the worst you could do
>   to me
>   was to take my life,
when my heart kept safely within my own chest,
when the threat to my flesh
>   was contained on my own
>   body. But now?

Now the days are just packed with gap-toothed smiles and
>   sneak-attack hugs, whole mornings of either rambling
>   tweenage stories
>   of queered up Rick Riordan fanfic
>   or a seven-year old's Minecraft youtube channel reviews,
hours of stream of consciousness jokes that never seem to land on a punchline
>   and teary-eyed bedtime requests and last-minute homework
questions and
>   simultaneously both too much and never quite enough ice
cream.

These days became my life.

It was a good life
and like Neo I was beginning

to believe.

But you have left nothing to believe in—
or rather
there is nothing I can risk believing in. A hungry man is
an angry man,
but a frightened parent
>   is a scary motherfucker.

The old version of me could never dream
of all I would do to pull one smile across tiny quivering lips,
pluck nightmares from tired minds like nits from unwashed fur,
to be so convincing when I lie
        and promise them that they are safe,
        that Daddy can protect them,

that they can cuddle, and go to sleep, and I
will always be here when they wake.
They don't like it when I leave the house, you see, and I am unsure how
        to explain that I take each step as if
        all streets were built of razorblades, as if
        all rooftops hide a sniper, as if
        each siren secretly a death poem.
I thought I knew hate, that I had it beaten when I was angry, when I was just me,
        before my wife and I became one, then
        two, now three.

But as you know hatred is hollow
without love to fill it
        and my soul has grown deep like the rivers and I had thought
        that would be a good thing. Nature abhors a vacuum, but
        your system detests fulfillment,

and we all know which side rules here.

It was easier to be angry and not afraid. The purest fear
is the unknown, and I do not know
what I could do,
all I could do,
all I would do,

I do not know who I could be,
> and I guess part of me will always hate the world you built

for forcing me to even ask these fucking questions.

12.

There are moments that
become poems, too perfect
to be left unsaid,

I twitch in that un—
bearable anxious space, wish—
ing it leaves a mark

to blossom into
this rose I cannot explain
that still explains me.

13.

The kids don't like it
when I listen to the news.
I have to sneak Rachel Maddow into the shower with me,
always be prepared to instantly switch from snarky
    analysis on The Root or mind-numbing number-crunching
    on *FiveThirtyEight*
    to Lionel Messi highlights,
and I keep *The Mandalorian* ready to pop up at a moment's notice so
    they don't see *The Daily Kos* sliding down on my screen.

This should not be normal.

I remember sitting wide-eyed beside my dad on the couch
as he explained who all the latest characters were in The Iran Hostage
    drama playing across our nightly broadcasts, or else listened
    patiently as Dad identified Carter Reagan Jesse Jackson and
    (lord help us all)
    Jim and Tammy Faye Baker.
Perry Farrell told us the news was
just another show, one we watched
the same way
    we watched anything else,

each episode would end and Walter Cronkite tell us
    "And that's the way it is,"
    and off we went to bed,
    good night.

But that was before a man with a camcorder spotted a King and
    his video disrupted everything, before the first Gulf War live-
    dropped precision guided missiles into
    the silos of impressionable teenage minds, before twin
    metal behemoths collapsed into showers of fire, a time when
    presidents still hid behind dog-whistles instead of screaming
    atop loudspeakers.

My kids don't like it when I listen to the news
       because they know that's
       where the bodies are,
       that's where their bodies are,

that's where every word is war
and they need no reminder
our side is losing.

14.

Hope, hope is a song you didn't realize you knew
        the words to until you dared to dance. Hope,
        hope is a belief

that when your time comes to stride to the front someone
        will be there having your back. Hope, hope
        births itself

in your imagination, feeds on your memory, and lodges
        within your chest like some gleeful parasite. Hope, hope
        is symbiotic and cathartic,
        helpful and helpless, lost and somehow still
        your guiding light.

It will blister fingers and twist
        in your hands, slip and fall
        if you grip too tight,
        if you let go,
        if you stare too hard,
        if you look away.

It has never existed, but
it's all we are made from.
Hope is a thing impossible to talk about
        without sounding corny or emotional.
        It is the thing most needing to be talked about.

My son told me that hope and compassion are the weakest
        emotions in these times and seven year olds should never
        have to be that observant, or that sad. I told him he
        was wrong, he
        could not be more wrong. Any person
        who can hold to hope,
        who can care even for others they do not know,
        who can believe this world
        somehow worthy of their effort,

such a person is to be feared, to be respected;
> a handful of such people scream down tyrants,
> build up governments,
> give birth to movements.

He listened, silent, and in his face I could see it.
> To be honest, only a touch.

But then again,
> just enough.

As a mixed-race child of the 80's, **Martin Wiley** grew up confronting and embracing a world as mixed and confused as he was, surrounded by beautiful words one minute and screamed hate the next. A long-time activist, spoken-word artist, and slam poet, after marrying the love of his life he settled down and saw his work shift back onto the page. After receiving a degree from Goddard College, he went on to receive his MFA from Rutgers Camden, where he was a Rutgers University Fellow. He had begun to see himself as a "recovering poet" but his children's growing love of words dragged him, mostly happily, off the wagon. Martin remains in Philadelphia, teaching, being a dad and husband, and finding time, when possible, to write.